Computers:
Literacy and
Learning

The Practicing Administrator's Leadership Series

Jerry J. Herman and Janice L. Herman, Editors

ROADMAPS
TO SUCCESS

Other Titles in the Series Include:

Computers: Literacy and Learning

A Primer For Administrators

George E. Marsh II

CORWIN PRESS, INC.
A Sage Publications Company
Newbury Park, California

For information address:

Corwin Press, Inc.
A Sage Publications Company
2455 Teller Road
Newbury Park, California 91320

SAGE Publications Ltd.
6 Bonhill Street
London EC2A 4PU
United Kingdom

SAGE Publications India Pvt. Ltd.
M-32 Market
Greater Kailash I
New Delhi 110 048 India

Printed in the United States of America

Library of Congress Cataloging-in-Publication Data

Marsh II, George E.
      Computers: literacy and learning : a primer for administrators /
George E. Marsh II.
           p.   cm. — (Roadmaps to success)
      Includes bibliographical references.
      ISBN 0–8039–6073–5 (pbk.)
      1. Computer-assisted instruction.   I. Title.   II. Series.
LB1028.5.M32   1993
371.3'34—dc20   93–22

93 94 95 96 10 9 8 7 6 5 4 3 2 1

Corwin Press Production Editor: Marie Louise Penchoen

Contents

Foreword

A lthough some of George Marsh's statements in this guide will appear controversial, we nevertheless believe that he presents a realistic set of concerns and challenges that should be considered seriously by educators. Without doubt, instruction can be delivered in a business-as-usual manner with technology. Equally without doubt, the information society is evolving rapidly and its supportive technological communication and information delivery systems are here to stay on our educational scene.

Marsh provides many specific examples of instructional uses of technology, and he details various hardware and software structures and processes. His listing of adaptive devices and instructional uses of technology for handicapped students is especially helpful and interesting. Practical student scenarios clearly demonstrate the multiple uses and advantages of student instruction aided by technology.

Technologically literate students are the goal, individual productive adult workers are the product, and successful U.S. competitive leadership in the world is the preferred visionary outcome.

JERRY J. HERMAN
JANICE L. HERMAN
Series Co-Editors

About the Author

George E. Marsh II is currently Professor of Computer Technology in the College of Education, the University of Alabama, Tuscaloosa. He is a past director of the college computer labs, and he helped establish the Center for Communications and Educational Technology on the Tuscaloosa campus, which now delivers numerous satellite courses to thousands of public-school students in the Southeast. His previous experience includes faculty positions at the University of Miami and the University of Arkansas, and teaching and administrative positions at both the elementary and secondary levels in public schools.

George Marsh has published numerous books and articles in education, including some of the first research involving computer-assisted instruction with microcomputers. He has contributed to the development of over 200 educational software programs, and of distance-education courses, via satellite and computers, at universities and in the Star Schools Project. As consultant to the United Nations, he guided the design of a tracking system for the postwar economic rehabilitation of Afghanistan. Currently, he is pursuing a program to revise pre-service teacher education that incorporates teaching competencies in the uses of technologies for communication, administration, and classroom instruction.

Introduction

Educational practice has always been influenced by economic and social forces. The current educational reform movement in the United States was inspired by fear of technological and economic inferiority to Japan and Europe. Noticing that Japanese and German companies were winning away world markets in consumer electronics, machine tools, and automobiles, business and political leaders in the United States recognized a shift away from an industrial economy dominated by American manufacture and export. Blaming American education instead of poor business planning for the economic decline, school reform measures were promulgated to restore American economic competitiveness by addressing perceived deficiencies in the educational system rather than by examining business policies. The foundation for school reform was the "Nation at Risk" report of 1983. Many reform measures in this document have since been implemented in many states and school districts. Although schools had been successfully meeting needs during the smokestack era, the postindustrial economy seemed to occur suddenly and represented a new kind of competition with vague rules.

According to Drucker (1989), the global economy is now "transnational . . . shaped mainly by money flows rather than by trade in goods and services" (p. 109). As in Japan, Taiwan, and a renewed Europe, workers everywhere must learn to handle telecommunications and computing, work with electronic networks, access on-line catalogs, use electronic circulation systems, and manage data on optical disks and CD ROMs. America must invest in research, development, capital equipment, technologies, and training to create a demand for high-paying jobs and to match the quality of foreign competition. Literacy can no longer be regarded simply as verbal and mathematical skills but must include technical competence.

In the new transnational economy production, land, labor, and even money are much less important than the intelligence and skills of workers. This is where the United States is lagging most seriously behind Japan and Europe. The most important jobs in a modern economy are based on technical education and information technology, jobs for which the vast majority of the current work force and new school graduates are unprepared. In coming to terms with the new realities of the global economy, the United States is confronted with an awesome task of retraining the work force and changing schools to assure that our citizens have skills and knowledge equivalent to international competitors. There is a new world standard, and we are falling behind.

Thurow (1992) describes the new global economy as a "telecommunications-computer-transportation-logistics revolution" that permits global sourcing and a world capital market (p. 16). The world is a "level playing field" because anyone and everyone has access to the same market. Competitive advantages held by wealthy nations are now diminished. Now "process technologies" and "brainpower" are more important than manufacturing, cheap labor, and natural resources. Japan and Taiwan have no size or important natural resources, but they have invested heavily in human capital to gain a competitive advantage. Japan is a net exporter, after first importing raw materials from all over the world. The United States had the most successful economy in the world for most of this century because it had no economic competition. Thurow warns that the United States must accept the fact it is no longer the only world economic power—America must learn to compete and must shed the illusion that it can still make the rules.

Schools are being prodded to embrace technology for school improvement. At the broadest level, the reason is explained by the visionary Alvin Toffler (1991):

> In a knowledge-based economy the most important domestic political issue is no longer the distribution (or redistribution) of wealth, but of the information and media that produce wealth. This is a change so revolutionary it cannot be mapped by conventional political cartography. The new wealth-creation system will compel politicians, activists, and political theorists—whether they still regard themselves as left-wing or right-wing, radical or conservative, feminist or traditionalist—to rethink all political ideas developed during the smokestack era. The very categories are now obsolete. . . . No nation can operate a 21st-century economy without a 21st-century electronic infrastructure, embracing computers, data communications, and the other new media. This requires a population as familiar with this informational infrastructure as it is with cars, roads, highways, trains, and the transportation infrastructure of the smokestack period. (pp. 368-369)

Our workers and our pupils are unfamiliar with the "informational infrastructure" that Toffler describes. Most of our children do not ever touch a computer at school, and if they do, it is for some purpose other than mastering the device or using it as a resource. There is a serious gap between new job requirements and the ability of Americans to perform them. Advances in science and technology have persistently raised literacy requirements; the economy depends on literate people. In the coming economic battle with Japan and Europe, the United States must graduate a majority of its students with high levels of literacy and technical knowledge. It is insufficient to reduce the dropout rate if graduates complete only a "general track" of studies. This will still leave America unprepared for the economic challenge. We must virtually eliminate dropouts, tracking, and the general track, and turn out the majority of school graduates with literacy and technical knowledge comparable to that of our competitors.

The new jobs of the information age require increasing literacy and technical competence and also the abilities to learn, to work independently, and to work cooperatively. Service-sector economy will account for 88% of all jobs by the year 2000, most of which will require significant experience with various forms of technology. Public schools are being asked by enthusiasts to incorporate technology in various forms in order to improve instruction and to give students valuable learning experiences with technologies.

Technology can be used to improve education and certainly students need to become more technologically literate, but we must avoid thinking that technology alone will be a "quick fix" for education's ills. The commitment to raise the standards of teaching and learning in all crucial subject areas and in all our schools must also be part of the effort to produce literate and technologically competent graduates able to compete with any in the world.

Ensuring That Students Learn About and From Computers

At a time when resources are scarce and there is a general demand for school reform, it is difficult for some to accept the premise that funds should be used for technology. But our greatest challenge as a society is to recognize the importance of computers and other electronic technologies as the dominant factors in the new global economy. The basis of the modern knowledge age and global economy is *information technology*, and advances in technology will permeate virtually every aspect of life. Everyone and everything will be connected by coaxial and fiber-optic cables, telephone lines, and satellite. New, faster, cheaper, and smarter software and hardware will be developed, moving the world into an age of unprecedented communications capabilities and affecting every institution. Educators are advocating that schools must base teaching and learning on technology.

Wagner (1982) has indicated that interest in media systems (including computers and satellites) is likely to continue in education for the foreseeable future, because developments will provide a new scope for media use and because costs will decrease. But education is labor-intensive, clearly indicated by the school budget in which three-fourths of the funds are for teachers' salaries and benefits. Switching to a capital-intensive system, where technology replaces personnel, may be more appealing in education if there can be a reduction in overall real costs and if productivity (as measured in terms of achievement or graduates) remains the same or increases. As in other industries where labor has been replaced by machinery, technology in education is "likely to become of greater rather than lesser interest in the future" (Wagner, 1982, p. 2). The school administrator must be aware of the variety of existing and emerging technologies, the types of applications, and the costs and efficacy of various uses.

Two general kinds of applications are readily apparent: administration and instruction. In administrative applications there is little mystery or confusion about how to use technologies for increased efficiency. There are many kinds of software and hardware applications used in American businesses that can simply be imitated in the public school office. Thus various types of computers, software, and other innovations need only be transplanted.

This is not true, however, with instructional applications. As long as teachers are trained in traditional college programs and receive their professional internships in traditional school settings, the use of technology in the classroom will probably not make much difference in teaching and learning. The predominant model of classroom instruction in teacher training (Rosenshine & Stevens, 1986) is based on group methods presumed to be effective: eye contact, types of questions, pauses, examples, and redirection of questions provided by the teacher. As practiced in most classrooms, group instruction is highly ineffective, especially compared to group instruction in Asian schools. Bloom (1984) advocates replacing group instruction with mastery learning or tutorial instruction, similar to instruction in Asian schools, according to reports of Stevenson and Stigler (1992). Mastery learning results in achievement one standard deviation above a traditional class. Tutorial instruction (one teacher to four or fewer students) exceeds traditional classes by two standard deviations! Bloom contends that 98% of all children in public schools could achieve at high levels with tutorial instruction. In large classrooms, however, tutorial instruction is only possible with computers.

Although opportunity (time) is considered an important predictor of learning, the amount of time allotted for instruction is not as important as the content and processes of instruction. Off-task behavior of a student is no more deleterious to learning than on-task behavior devoted to inappropriate content. The most important component is evaluation (requiring students to pass a level of learning before moving on to the next level). Frequent evaluation is highly related to achievement. It forces the teacher and students to attend to mastery as well as to sequential skills.

For the typical teacher—trained as a group instructor—individual learning is tactically impossible. Individualization presents several problems:

- Individualization is too demanding of a teacher's time— simply organizing instruction by objectives for a single class or subject matter requires additional effort.
- Individualization requires extraordinary record keeping.
- Individualization fails because teachers are incapable of collecting the required information.
- Individualization cannot exist without evaluation.

The fact that these steps must be done daily for each pupil is why teachers cannot provide adequate instruction. Most teachers do not attempt it. As Bloom indicated, the more nearly instruction approaches a tutorial model, the greater the achievement level for the class and each individual. Technology is the only way to provide better education for pupils by increasing individualization, performing assessment, and approaching tutorial instruction.

Educators have never embraced technology or media in classrooms. Media has been perceived negatively by teachers and considered disruptive to classroom harmony (Dodge et al., 1974). Teachers rarely use any form of media, including overhead transparencies, models, tapes, videos, or pictures in books and magazines (Heinich, Molenda, & Russell, 1989).

Rejection of technology by teachers is related to the predominant teaching model—group instruction—which benefits only students with the most aptitude. Technology is perceived negatively by teachers because they view it as an additional burden.

Rather than making group instruction more efficient, which is what the teacher has been trained to do, the teacher must significantly alter the physical space of the classroom and change customary routines. If computers are to be effectively used in classroom instruction, each teacher will have to be trained how to use the technology and will have to accept a different role as "facilitator" of learning (see below).

The capabilities of the computer as a multimedia tool, an individual tool, and the hub of small-group activities are only important if such applications can increase achievement. If integration of technology with the school curriculum is to become a reality, teachers must learn how to use technology in the classroom, not as another group instructional device but as an inherent part of the system of the educational process.

Several questions might be addressed about the effects of computer instruction, as they should about any innovation, such as the skills needed by teachers and pupils, subjects where applications will be most useful, ways to improve classroom activities, the kind of supervision required, and maintenance (see Chapter 3). Administrators quite naturally want to know how to get the most for investment of their available resources, so articles in educational research frequently appear about such important issues. For example, should schools group youngsters by ability? Should schools use a particular organizational pattern, such as a middle school? Similarly, questions have been raised about using money to purchase computer equipment when it might be used for other school needs.

While the popularity of technology in education enjoys a renaissance, American education is entering a new phase of computer use known as "curriculum integration." The goal of technology use advocates that all teachers in elementary and secondary programs use computers in every aspect of the curriculum. A kind of "shared pedagogy" that meets the needs of teachers and learners is emerging in American education. Perelman (1991) reported on a number of "restructuring" schools throughout the nation, citing these characteristics:

- Schools invest in equipment and tools necessary to increase productivity and effectiveness in the classroom.

- Students do not receive information passively; instead, they are engaged in project-oriented activities that result in projects or exhibitions.
- Students use the tools of knowledge production to create their own products.
- Students use telecommunications to make weekly television programs that are distributed on the school's network.
- Students use on-line services, video conferencing, and distance education within their own classrooms.
- Students engage in programs that promote personal learning goals.
- Cooperative learning becomes the norm.
- Classrooms are changing into workrooms and desks into workstations.

The trend is for pupils to be *constructivist* learners, a notion expressed in the Piagetian view of learning. As pupils become more responsible for their own learning, there is a parallel trend in teacher training called *reflective teaching*, which is an attempt both to adjust teaching styles to integration of technology and to shift the burden from the teacher to the student for learning. This view of the teacher is more comprehensive than teacher as "manager," "technician," "academician," or "therapist." The reflective teacher (or "facilitator" of learning) is a decision maker who possesses the knowledge, skills, and beliefs to make decisions about the goals, strategies, and educational consequences of teaching. Reflective teachers would use three types of reflection—technical, practical, and critical (Kemmis, 1985).

The reflective teacher does not transmit facts about a subject but seeks to make students able to understand concepts and conduct inquiry in a given field (constructivism). This type of teaching skill can only develop as teachers reflect about ways that students interact with subject matter. This reflection leads teachers to explore the implications of theories for teaching and the mastery of subject matter knowledge by students. Pedagogical representations of disciplinary knowledge are nowhere cataloged, and their study has only recently begun. Lacking a clear base for making the change, teachers must be able to implement a variety of instructional models. Because important interactions between models of teaching and student achievement in different kinds of subject matter are known to exist, teachers must be capable of assessing a range of models and strategies as they apply to a teaching field. Recitation, direct instruction, mastery learning, cooperative learning, divergent models, and individualized instruction are but a few of the models of teaching that teachers must be capable of performing. Teachers must also be able to use a broad range of instructional media and techniques, including computer-based instructional technologies.

As noted by Wagner (1982), "The problem with any labour cost is that it is always rising. In contrast, improved technology leads to the reduction of unit capital costs. So even from a starting position in which labour is cheap and capital expensive, the unit costs move in opposite directions—labor upwards and capital downwards. The point at which they intersect depends on many factors, but in the long run the use of more capital (which largely means media) as a substitute for labour in education becomes increasingly attractive" (p. 2).

Education in the United States and other industrialized nations is on the bottom rung of the technology ladder that, once the ascent begins, may lead to reduced overall costs, improved teacher salaries, professionalization of education, better achievement, and a healthier economy. But whether or not any of these outcomes are realized depends on decisions made by administrators, training of teachers, and continued evaluation of the effectiveness of specific kinds of informational technologies in teaching for specific skills and knowledge. Initial capital outlays may not culminate in immediate benefits. Appropriate technology must be strategically used to achieve specific objectives, some of which may have economic consequences.

Technologies can be used to improve education, improve working conditions, and support the missions of the school. Collins (1991) has noted the shifts in American schools as technology has been introduced. Some of these shifts are summarized here:

A shift from whole-class to small-group instruction has occurred, based on the use of computers. Students are able to move at their own rates and teachers can provide individualized instruction, too. According to Collins, one study resulted in a reduction of whole-class instruction from 70% to 10% of the time with an appreciable increase in teachers spending time with individuals. This may be a humanizing effect of computers in education.

A shift from lecturing to coaching has taken place. The major benefit here is that children become more self-reliant, generate their own questions and hypotheses, and begin to develop a constructivist approach to learning rather than viewing the teacher as the font of all knowledge.

A greater amount of time is given to task and engagement. Computers enable the student to spend more time in learning activities and to become interested in learning. Engagement, as opposed to just performing tasks, means that students begin to enjoy the process of learning, with the result that boredom diminishes.

Performance assessment rather than summative tests is being used. Partly because students can develop papers faster with computers—freed from the slowness of a pencil—teachers are able to construct tasks that require elaborate products. Teams or individual students can produce work that is evaluated as a product rather than as discrete skills.

Cooperative learning is on the rise. Cooperative learning has been a growing trend in education for several years. The computer in the classroom makes cooperative work easier and reduces individual competitiveness of students. Viewed as a social or cognitive variable, cooperative work is becoming more important in the global economy and is a value that is being taught in classrooms to prepare workers of the future.

When microcomputers were first introduced in educational programs, there were many skeptics and detractors. At first it was easy to resist computers because of the poor quality of instructional software. When schools adopted "computer literacy goals" based on programming in Logo or BASIC—either as an elective course or a general requirement—microcomputers and software came under the control of a "computer teacher" in a "computer lab," which effectively kept computers out of mainstream classrooms. Now there exists a critical mass of "schools of the future" and "magnet schools" throughout the nation having significant experience using computers in all subject areas in which computers are standard equipment (O'Malley, 1989), and there is a genuine trend to introduce computers into all classrooms.

A spectacular example is cited by Gross (1989) of the dropout rate being stemmed in a Maryland school through the use of computers. Focusing on one school that had been ranked 12th among 24 in the district, after intervention with computers the school ranked 3rd. Most remarkable were the results that the average reading-level score of 8th graders was 11th grade and 10th grade for mathematics. The average IQ was reported as 107; 92% of the children in the school had scores above the national norms. Results such as these are most encouraging for the successful application of technology in schools.

Computers in Schools: The Most Commonly Asked Questions

Simply placing computers in classrooms without a plan or a strategy will not be productive in most settings. Many questions have to be addressed in preparation for integrating computers with the curriculum. The curriculum itself may be changed as a result of the increased capabilities made possible by the technology. The fundamental questions of why and how, and the details of integration, are treated in subsequent chapters. Here are some of the most frequently encountered general questions raised by teachers unfamiliar with technology.

What should teachers know?

Requiring teachers to learn how to program computers was one of the biggest errors in educational computing. This set the expectation that computers were for programming, which has since been reinforced by an entire specialty field—keeping computers in labs that are controlled by "computer teachers" who teach programming to pupils. What we need now are teachers who know how to integrate computers and use available software in their classrooms in whatever subjects they teach. Some college programs are beginning to shift toward training teachers to use a computer as a tool (word processing, spreadsheet, database), as a multimedia device, and as a means of supporting instructional goals. Unfortunately, these goals will have to be the responsibility of in-service programs in a district.

Where should computers be placed?

If there are only a few computers in the school, they will have to be shared, unless they are assigned specifically to certain programs or classrooms. Otherwise, the trend is clearly to place as many computers in classrooms as possible, stand-alone or networked, so that teachers and students may use them frequently. Computers in a media center or a lab restrict access and make computers unimportant to the regular class routines.

Who has responsibility for teaching about computers?

The role of the "computer teacher" may change from teaching programming instruction to a select few to teaching all students how to use a computer. The computer must be considered both as an object of study and a tool to help students learn in other courses of the curriculum. Decisions have to be made about what tool skills students should have and who should teach them. Any computer user today should know basic information about operating a computer and should master an integrated package composed of a word processor, database, and spreadsheet. Whoever has responsibility for these computer-teaching tasks must be able to relinquish authority to classroom teachers to use computers in various areas of the curriculum; computers should be used much as a pencil is now used in classrooms. It is essential that some plan be developed to teach all students how to use the computer as a tool and the proper use and care of equipment and software, and that a separate plan be developed for those students who will learn programming or advanced uses of the computer.

What goals and objectives should be addressed by the classroom teacher?

This question has as many answers as there are classrooms. To the extent that a teacher has leeway in making such decisions, the needs of the teacher for instruction and the needs of the students for access must be balanced with the available equipment and with some list of priorities for instruction. In mathematics and science classrooms, students should have access to computers and appropriate software for teaching and for solving equations or performing simulations. In all classrooms, students should have access to databases and other information sources. In schools and classrooms where computers are available for general classroom use, the teacher can incorporate the computer as an instructional tool and a support tool.

Who should teach keyboarding skills and when should they be taught?

Many activities and instructional programs do not require typing skills. If students are expected to complete papers, reports, and other printed materials, they must have the necessary training. Some schools teach formal typing or "keyboarding" to children as early as the third grade.

What teaching strategies are required to use a computer in the classroom?

In reality, the computer is just a tool—a very powerful multimedia tool—that can be used with any strategy the teacher may employ, from lecture presentations to individual work.

What about maintenance?

Proper care of equipment and software is essential. The school should have a plan for repairing equipment. There are many ways to do this, but some districts have found it cost-effective to have some professional person trained to do certain kinds of simple repairs so computers can be kept running. Most basic kinds of problems and troubleshooting are within the scope of classroom teachers if they are trained.

Who has responsibility for cataloging and shelving software?

This is a difficult problem, especially with floppies. It makes little sense to plan a lesson for students with particular software in mind if you cannot be certain the software will be available when you need it. Many teachers have limited the use of films in their classes for this very reason. It takes extraordinary advanced planning to make sure that equipment and films are reserved well in advance of when they are needed. Schools may want to use a particular package with several students but may not have sufficient funds to provide the necessary copies. Some companies have created programs to permit schools to make their own duplicates at the local level. In network versions of software, the same advantages exist.

The Best Uses of Computers

Overcoming Resistance to Technology

The administrator must recognize that technology can be undermined by teachers whose traditional roles are changing. Technology threatens teachers' status, changes the way work is accomplished, and strikes at teachers' basic autonomy in the classroom. It is critical that teachers first use technology to make present teaching practices easier and more efficient, beginning with ways that teachers themselves find the technology most useful. With the passage of time, an evolutionary process can unfold wherein teachers are eager to shift to instruction delivered *by* technology.

There is reason to believe that teachers will become enthusiastic after having some experience. Higgins (1990) studied 1,100 computer-using teachers and found these results:

- 64% believed that computers reduced the dropout rate.
- 91% believed reading and writing skills improved with computer use.
- 40% believed that computers helped in math instruction more than in any other subject.
- 62% believed that computer use decreased discipline problems.

Dwyer, Ringstaff, and Sandholtz (1991) have reported that teachers who had regular access to computer technology in their classrooms over several years experienced significant changes in their instructional styles. The main change was that teachers at the elementary and secondary levels moved away from competitive work patterns toward collaborative work patterns—the new trend necessary for knowledge workers in the information age. Used properly, the computer can significantly increase achievement, reduce negative effects of large class size, improve self-esteem of the learner, and make school more interesting. It can also allow for more individualized teaching, tutorial instruction, and collaborative work. Schools are experimenting with changing the process of instruction, redefining the roles of teacher and students in the learning process, and shifting more responsibility for instruction to technology.

Schools in the United States have steadily purchased microcomputers for instructional uses and by 1989 had reached the following ratios of pupils per computer: 36.8 to 1 in elementary school, 27.6 in junior high, 26.3 in senior high, and 30.8 overall (Office of Technology Assessment, 1989). Also, 90% of schools have videocassette players, each state has educational television, and many districts are developing electronic communications networks. Computers are accessible primarily in labs and are used for drill in Chapter I programs, programming instruction under the direction of "computer teachers," and business education. Few classroom teachers use computers in teaching. Most pupils do not use computers frequently at all.

Not only is the lab an obstacle to computer use by classroom teachers but so is the culture of teaching. The principal method of instruction in American education is whole-group instruction. The curriculum, classroom, textbooks, and teaching methodologies are predicated on group instruction. All major research traditions in education are based on a search for the best method of group instruction (Bloom, 1984). From junior high school through graduate school, the majority of instruction is accomplished through lecture.

Teaching effectiveness is judged according to criteria for skills in group management, including the handling of disruptive behavior, and for presenting information and questioning pupils appropriately. As long as the teacher's primary role is to deliver instruction by lecture and ask questions of students, a role reinforced and rewarded by the system, the productivity of education will not increase.

Should Schools Use Computers?

School personnel continually question the use of computers in classrooms. Teachers and patrons may argue that money spent on technology should be used for teacher salaries and supplies, and they will question the effectiveness of computer instruction, despite a growing body of supporting research. In fact, for over a decade it has been known that computer-assisted instruction is effective in meeting specific learning objectives, there is a 20%-40% time saving in learning, retention rates are equal or superior to conventional instruction, and students enjoy using computers. Niemiec, Blackwell, and Walberg (1986) reported that, compared to peer tutoring, adult tutoring, and smaller class size, an average CAI (computer-assisted instruction) program produces greater gains per $100 of expenditure. The Office of Technology Assessment (1989) reported the following:

- Elementary children who use computers show gains in achievement between 1 and 8 months higher than non computer using peers.
- Microcomputer-based labs have proven that children can grasp complex concepts and master analytical techniques.
- Students who use databases outperform controls in tests of information-processing skills.
- Normal and learning-disabled students who use word processors make significant improvement in writing.
- Reading comprehension can be improved with computer-aided reading programs that focus on comprehension and the whole text.

Walberg (1991) examined 377 research studies, selected according to criteria for quality of research designs, that had compared computer-assisted instruction with conventional classroom instruction. Seeking to compare educational methods for difference in effects on learning, he found in all cases that computer-assisted instruction combined with classroom teaching was superior to classroom instruction without computer assistance. The computer was found to be particularly effective with the handicapped, elementary students, and secondary students.

How Can Computers Be Used?

Computers can be used in the classroom in endless ways, but school organization, curriculum, and budget influence decisions about computer use. Uses may be different where children receive most instruction from one or two teachers or where the curriculum has a departmental approach. Where subjects become the central organizing feature of the curriculum, different strategies may be employed. The *best* use of computers must be determined according to each situation. There is no simple answer, because possible uses and best uses depend not only on the factors above but also on the values, philosophy, and goals of the school system.

The greatest obstacle to the use of computers is the institutional model of putting computers into labs. A pattern reinforced by both curriculum requirements for pupils and certification requirements for teachers in many states, the computer lab puts access beyond the reach of classroom teachers and makes the use of computers a special event. In order for computers to be used widely throughout the curriculum, they must be put into classrooms for use across the curriculum (Kozma & Johnston, 1991).

Computers can be used in schools in a variety of ways:

- One-Computer Classroom
- Low-Density Computerized Classroom
- High-Density Computerized Classroom
- Networked Classroom
- Computer Lab
- Networked School

A description of each type of usage follows below.

The One-Computer Classroom

Many schools have at least one computer in the classroom. Typically, the computer is used by the teacher as a means of collecting and maintaining administrative records for the classroom and the school, as a personal tool for the teacher, and for some instructional activities. The teacher may use the computer for correspondence, report generation, and typical "office" activities.

Some teachers use one computer as a way to present information for group activities. Any microcomputer can be equipped with a special overhead projector that transfers images on the computer screen to the overhead screen. A teacher may also use a videodisc player, CD-ROM player, and printer to provide lessons more conveniently. In effect, this use is as a *multimedia* device to support the teacher in instruction.

A variation of this is the "itinerant" or "nomad" computer that is rolled into a classroom on a cart for specific applications and activities. With a good schedule for borrowing, teachers can plan to use the computer effectively for presentation of classroom instruction and some limited use by students. Careful planning and reliability in scheduling are crucial, because teachers must know they can count on the computer being there for a planned lesson.

A permanent computer in the classroom provides the teacher with more flexibility in planning for its use. Students know where it is and can use it easily any time the teacher or activities dictate. The teacher can plan both individualized and cooperative learning activities and can supervise the students. A disadvantage may be that the computer may not be used all the time, while there will be other classrooms needing computers. From the principal's point of view, this may appear to be a waste of resources. Teachers who have a computer for instructional purposes need to keep it busy, especially if they want to justify further purchases of computers. A problem with the computer in the classroom may be that software must be shared among several classrooms. The teacher may spend a lot of time working out arrangements with other teachers to acquire software for the correct times.

The mobile computer can be used in a similar way, except that teachers tend not to rely on a computer being available and will gradually leave it out of lesson plans and activities. Moving a computer about from place to place also increases the potential for accidental damage and loss of software.

The Low-Density Computerized Classroom

In a low-density classroom, the teacher may have a ratio of 6 or more students to 1 computer. A classroom with this arrangement is highly suitable for a variety of instructional models, depending on the subject matter and the teaching style of the instruction.

The computer-to-student ratio is not great enough to allow planning for several highly individualized daily activities, but there may be significant individualized and small group activities. The key to using computers in this arrangement, and in the high-density and networked classrooms, is to conceptualize the computer as a central feature of a work station to employ combinations of teacher-directed activities using the capabilities of current software. The computer, in almost all subject-matter areas, will have several general applications (described below).

The applications can be applied in a computer lab or media center, a classroom with one computer, or in other classrooms that have many computers, including the rare school that has networked computers in the classrooms. These applications can be used by virtually any teacher, in some combination, as an individual tool, a group instructional device, and for increasingly individualized instruction or group work, such as cooperative learning activities.

Word Processing

Although the word processor is a tool for writing, it can be used in all classrooms for generating reports and completing other written assignments. It may be particularly well suited to some classes in language arts or English. Not all students will be capable of typing, of course, which will limit its uses in this respect. But those who can should be encouraged to use it under rules and guidelines established by the teacher. Nonetheless, research has indicated that students not only enjoy creating their own reports, poems, and articles on computers but they actually feel freer, just like adults, because the tedious process of making corrections is easier with word processing than with pencil or pen.

Almost any classroom, especially in later elementary, middle school, junior high, and high school, can use computers for word-processing activities. Even in small group arrangements, one student with typing skills can collate all the written work of students in a cooperative learning project and type the report.

Computers can be used to support writing assignments in all subjects and in language arts in particular. Tools available include outlines, on-line databases, drafting, text-analysis tools, graphics, spelling and grammar "checkers," and built-in functions for references and cross-references. It may be that the very existence of computers and word-processing software will cause new types of writing to emerge, freed of constraints set by the typewriters and print of the last generation.

One such new type of writing is *collaborative writing*, which is made possible because of the computer. More than one writer may share files, electronic mail, bulletin boards, and network dialogues. This may not only relieve the "loneliness" of writing but also promote cooperative learning and sharing, important activities in the new economy. Rather like adults as they prepare for a speech before an audience even if they know the content well, pupils who write to "electronic" pen pals on a network take greater care in their preparation and constructions.

Database Management

The database and spreadsheet features can be employed for many problems confronted in many classrooms, including not only mathematics and science but also foreign language, social studies, English, literature, health, and almost any other subject area. Rather than being tools solely for businesses to calculate potential profits or generate mailing labels, spreadsheets and databases are valuable tools in many disciplines.

Databases can be used by the teacher for general instructional purposes for the group and can be used by students individually and in small work groups. In general, besides being used as a way to manage information, the database can be used for hypothesis testing. For example, one high school teacher collected census data from New York City on Irish immigrants at the turn of the century and had students enter and sort the data. He then asked them to answer several questions. In this particular case, he had 4 to 5 students for each computer, using the AppleWorks database. After actively discussing problems with the data, generating hypotheses, and then searching the database, the students learned much more about the Irish immigrants than would have ordinarily occurred by simply reading the conclusion, already written for them in a textbook. These conclusions thus became the students' conclusions, and they were able to defend them against challenges by showing the reports they had generated.

There are obviously many potential applications for this kind of activity in other areas of the curriculum. Health, history, and other areas provide students with real-world problems to assist in meeting the educational goals of the curriculum and the outcomes expected by the teacher. When students spend a lot of time generating hypotheses, manipulating data, and drawing conclusions, they develop greater insight and retain information longer than with less interactive methods.

Spreadsheet

To many people disinterested in business, the spreadsheet sounds like a cold, boring subject. However, the spreadsheet is actually an intellectual tool for analysis, prediction, interpretation, and even arithmetic or advanced mathematics applications. The spreadsheet can be used in science and mathematics classes, obviously, but it also has generic use in other areas of the curriculum. By putting numbers into rows and columns, the spreadsheet, with appropriate formulas entered, can do virtually any kind of data manipulation. Therefore, it can be used as a device for drawing conclusions, making inferences, and mastering a body of knowledge.

Understanding the concept of time is not mastered by most children until the age of 10 or 11, and then the concept of infinity or geologic time is difficult to grasp. In a series of exercises for a science class, students may be asked to enter and calculate problems in time and distance from school to different parts of the nation and the world, with different vehicles at various speeds, and then to imagine travel to distant planets or more remote galaxies. Simply by engaging in this type of activity, the students' concept of time is expanded. The concept of a vector can also be introduced concretely because students can see the differences of variables that are hard to describe or experience otherwise.

For example, hypothetical traveling from home to various planets and calculating the student's age at arrival on each planet gives insight about the great differences in distance and the vastness of space. In social studies, having the data from voting behavior of people broken down demographically provides students with concrete understanding of the differences in political attitudes and how they interact with wealth, race, geography, religion, and other factors.

Drill

Drill can be beneficial for some students who need to overlearn content, and it may be useful to all students on many aspects of a curriculum in which overlearning is essential. The use of drill is discussed in Chapter 5. Teachers may not use this application much, but it can be a valuable tool under the guidance of an experienced teacher.

Tutorial Instruction

This is a method that is highly useful for mastery of a concept and can be used by students in many subjects. The computer can provide actual assessment of a student's responses and learning, then make a variety of adjustments to assist the learner, much as a human tutor would attempt to do. The extent to which the teacher elects to use this method will depend on many variables, such as the number of computers available, the availability of software, the time allotted for instruction, and the attitude of the principal.

Simulation

This is a powerful use of the computer for group presentations and individualized learning activities. The simulation is a simulated real-life experience. Many sophisticated simulations give trainees the experience of flying an airplane or performing surgery. As schools begin to rely more on computers for instruction, more simulation software may become available for teachers to employ in classrooms, such as software that would give students real-life experiences that require the use of applied mathematics or science.

Telecommunications

Some classrooms may permit students to communicate with other classrooms in the building or district via modem and to engage in correlated learning activities with students in another state. Also, telecommunications permits search of bulletin boards and use of other services that may be beneficial to students in learning activities approved by the teacher.

The High-Density Computerized Classroom

A high-density classroom has a computer ratio of 4 or fewer pupils to each computer. These might be networked or stand-alone units. When a teacher has access to a high-density environment, virtually any kind of computer activity described above can be planned, and highly individual records can be maintained on students, including records of use, comparisons, and other kinds of research reported by the computer about the learning behavior and responses of students.

The Networked Classroom

A networked classroom may be the computer lab or other classrooms. Networked labs have the advantage of eliminating disk handling and can provide considerable management of computer activities. Depending on the controlling software and other options, many kinds of activities can be planned.

The obvious advantage of the network is the availability of software on the computer, which eliminates the need for finding software, booting machines, installing software, and so forth. The teacher does not have to keep a constant inventory and make sure students are handling disks properly and putting them back when they are finished.

The Computer Lab

Most schools still have computer labs. Except in those districts and states where state certification requirements demand that computer programming be under the supervision of a certified computer science teacher, classroom teachers can plan to use the lab to meet the instructional needs of a particular class.

If the lab is a media center in the library, there can be problems depending on the procedures and personnel involved. In the case of a librarian who treats the materials as books, with special requirements for checking them out, a lot of instructional time can be wasted. This has implications for small-group and cooperative-learning activities.

The Networked School

Although still rare, some schools are investing in networking buildings to take advantage of the power and savings of this arrangement. Networked schools can exponentially increase the communications and educational uses of computers. Students can access information in the library, even when they are not in the library, and can use printers and other devices not physically present in a particular classroom. The local-area network expands the power of computers, spreads out the costs of software, and turns individual computers into a communications and file-sharing network.

Integrating Computers with Classroom Instruction

Once it as been determined how computers can be used in a given situation, they must be specifically integrated with classroom instruction. As we have seen, the possibilities are endless. Among the variables governing integration are the policies of the school, the curriculum, the teacher's philosophy, the availability of computers and software, and the competency of the teacher to use computers for specific purposes.

Integration can be conceptualized as technological delivery (as media or methodology) in lesson plans developed by the teacher. The teacher may examine both the units of instruction and the software available to make a series of lesson plans. Lesson plans probably follow a specific format at each school, but most of them have certain characteristics in common, such as a statement of the subject, the learning objective, the instructional activity, the outcomes expected, performance indicators, and the materials and equipment to be used.

Here are the major integrative uses of the computer in the classroom:

- Personal productivity for teachers and pupils

- Adaptive/augmentation uses for exceptional students
- Multimedia instruction
- Support for the teacher
- Telecommunications

The first four uses are described below. Telecommunications functions are described in Chapter 6.

Personal Productivity

The major productivity applications for the computer are word processing, database, and spreadsheet. Teachers and pupils can use all three of these applications as the basis for school-related work.

Word Processing

Word processing can be used by pupils in all aspects of the curriculum, not just writing. A popular word-processing program for IBM and MS-DOS computers is *WordPerfect*. Popular programs for Macintosh are *MacWrite* and *Microsoft Works*. A common word-processing program in many schools for the Apple II series is *AppleWorks*. All of these programs are similar, differing only in complexity and features.

Teaching children keyboarding can begin as early as the 3rd grade, and when children can type 25 words per minute, they can use the word processor effectively. Some people object to teaching young children to type, particularly business teachers who believe that poor skills will be difficult to correct later. For now, keyboarding is the foundation for all other computer applications, except computer-assisted instruction, and inability to type is a serious limitation. Soon it will be possible to control word processing by speech commands rather than keystrokes.

A dynamic feature of word processing is the capability to automatically check and correct misspelled words in a document. This, too, like the calculator, is controversial with some educators, who believe that children who use spell checking will not learn to spell the words themselves and will become dependent on the spell checker. There is no definitive research on this topic, and it could be that children who use the spell checker actually learn to spell better than they would without it. An undisputed advantage of word processing, however, is the availability of a thesaurus.

Word processing has affected the writing curriculum, particularly creative writing. There is no guarantee that pen, pencil, or word processing will stimulate creativity, but writing in any medium can be a tedious process. Saving time and permitting experimentation—with the ability to save, copy, delete, replace, and so forth—motivate children to write. When pupils learn to keyboard, writing becomes cognitive rather than psychomotor. They can write for the sake of learning to write, and they can use word processing as a general tool to assist them in all of their areas of study within the curriculum.

Database

As a basic productivity tool, the database has become useful to students in most areas of the curriculum and to teachers at any level or subject. A database can be used to show students the complexity of information and how apparently unrelated data are actually connected. Databases can be used in social science, science, mathematics, fine arts, or any area of the curriculum.

A database is a collection of information stored in a computer that can be queried to answer certain questions. In business and government applications the usefulness of the database is readily apparent. The data can be organized and searched in different ways to provide specific information of interest. Databases save a lot of time, such as printing mailing labels or making flight reservations. Searching for particular flights, with certain accommodations, at specific times, with the cheapest fare, would be almost impossible to do by hand. A database of airline flights and ticket prices is worth more than an airline fleet.

The simplest way to conceptualize a database is as a file cabinet full of records. Folders are used to keep data on transactions, events, and personal information about students. Each collection of folders is called a *file*; each individual folder is a *record*. Each record contains one or more pieces of information called *categories* or *fields* (for example, name, address, and so forth). Each specific item in a category is called an *entry*. Stored electronically, the fields can be organized and searched in specific ways to provide quick answers to questions.

A number of educational uses of databases have been developed, such as the *States* database, the *British Monarchs*, and the *Presidents Database*. In the latter, all important data for each president are entered into fields, such as party membership, position before presidency, dates in office, date of death, vice president's name, and so forth. Students are asked to answer many types and levels of questions, and, in the process, they learn not only a great deal about the U.S. presidents but also about how to use a database.

A social studies teacher obtained data from county records about the ages, occupations, and causes of death for people in the county at different times throughout the century. Students were able to see how life expectancy has increased, how young many people were at the time of death at the turn of the century, and that certain kinds of diseases either do not exist today or are no longer life threatening.

In a scientific experiment, one girl had friends, relatives, and pen pals provide her with the pH and chlorine content of water from several cities and regions, all collected within the same time frame. Through analysis on the database, she was able to generate an interesting report about water quality across several regions.

Some software programs and books introduce children to a database with exercises on planets or dinosaurs because there are few fields and entries. In one exercise, there are only 6 fields and 14 records (one for each kind of dinosaur included). After the data are entered into a database, questions can be asked. For example, using the correct commands, a student might ask the questions, "What relationships are there among dinosaurs who lived in water?" "Among those who lived on land?" "Among those who did not have claws?" By entering the correct fields, the database is searched (queried) to sort out all dinosaurs who lived on land, then who lived on water, then with claws, and so forth. The information reveals itself, and it prompts considerable thinking on the part of students.

The database has great utility in most classrooms. Pupils, who may find data about certain subjects to be boring, will enjoy the ability to search data sets looking for answers to questions. They will begin to generate hypotheses about the data and then proceed to ask the necessary questions to confirm or deny each hypothesis.

Because setting up and searching a database can require thoughtful planning, a database can be a tool to introduce problem solving at virtually all levels in Bloom's taxonomy and can promote high-order thinking skills. A database search can require students to use questioning strategies encompassing the rules of logic. Skills taught with databases include the following:

- Finding differences and commonalities among events or data
- Analyzing relationships
- Looking for evidence of trends
- Generating and testing a hypothesis
- Organizing and structuring information
- Entering and retrieving data
- Synthesizing data
- Drawing inferences

Spreadsheet

Often regarded as a tool for accountants, the spreadsheet is adaptable to many areas of the curriculum but is particularly useful in science and mathematics. To use a spreadsheet a student must employ *logical* and *arithmetic operators* used in scientific formulas (for example, logical [=, <, >, < =, > –, < >] and arithmetic [+, –, *, /, ^]). Formulas can be written with actual values—as with a calculator—or may be used to manipulate cells.

The spreadsheet adds, subtracts, multiplies, divides, squares, extracts square roots, and so forth, by manipulation of cells. The formula, called an *argument*, requires the student to engage in considerable thought and planning. Teachers can use spreadsheets for teaching and keeping scores of students; older and advanced students may use them for almost any kind of mathematical and statistical calculations. Virtually any mathematics class in school from the elementary grades on could use a spreadsheet. It is a good way to introduce the concept of formulas to students, to get them to visualize solutions to problems, and to carefully check their data.

Formulas can be used to create rather complex sets of formulas connected to various cells in a spreadsheet. Usually this is done to solve a specific problem, but building complex sets of formulas is an important exercise in itself. As in the case of databases, spreadsheet activities can be used in many classes and at all age levels. Virtually any problem that can be asked in a class dealing with time, measurement, money, or distance, including algebra and calculus, can be put on a spreadsheet. Some students find that this makes the learning process more logical, concrete, and illustrative than simply working problems with a calculator or doing them on paper. Also, relationships not readily apparent in data sets can be revealed by means of spreadsheet activities.

Adaptive/Augmentation Uses

One of the greatest areas for applications of computers and related technologies is in the instruction and habilitation of handicapped pupils. The federal mandate has caused school systems to plan instructional materials and methods to meet the needs of exceptional pupils, which ever more frequently involves technology.

Computers are used with handicapped children in the same educational practices as other children: simulation, drill, tutorial instruction, word processing, and so forth. Some schools use computers to develop the Individualized Education Program (IEP) required for all handicapped students. In addition to instructional activities, computers and related technology can be used to habilitate the handicapped in many ways. IBM has supported the National Support Center for Persons with Disabilities in Atlanta, Georgia, which maintains a database of software packages and computer hardware for handicapped persons. Apple Corporation maintains a similar program, called the Apple Computer Clearing House. Currently, technology is used for instructional planning, communication, problem solving, and prosthetic devices.

IEP Software

The development of Individualized Education Programs (IEPs) for the handicapped is required by law. Similar programs are now required for preschool children and for adults who are placed in vocational or postsecondary education settings. The *Automated IEP System* and the *Comprehensive IEP Management System* are two examples. These programs permit the use of a stored database of objectives and entry of new objectives.

Adaptive Aids

Several types of adapted keyboards and alternative devices re-place keyboards and the mouse. Children missing hands or certain fingers and those with poor motor control need evaluation and proper outfitting. The *Dvork* keyboard was designed for one-handed users. The *Footmouse* is a cursor control operated by foot. *Mouthsticks* controlled by tongue movement and *Eyegaze* con-trolled by eye-operated commands, and other alternatives such as *Eyebrow* and *Finger Flex* switches that react to muscle movements, enable most any handicapped person to operate a computer.

RealVoice responds to a keyboard and creates human speech in a male or female voice. *Touchscreen* devices respond to simple touches of the monitor screen to control a computer program. The *Braille TeleCaption System* provides news, weather, sports, and education-al television programming for deaf-blind persons by translating news into Grade 1 Braille on printer paper. *Telephone Devices for the Deaf* (TDDs) are special modems attached to the computer via tele-phone lines so deaf persons can send and receive written messages.

Mobility

There are many kinds of mobility-related software and hard-ware to assist the visually impaired. The products have been de-veloped by mobility specialists.

Speech Synthesizers

Synthesizers are available to generate intelligible speech pro-duced by computers and other output devices. By pushing particular icons or typing on a keyboard the person with a communication disorder may engage in conversation. Children with no speech or labored speech are able to use synthesizers to communicate with others and to participate in the entire curriculum.

Visually Impaired

Screen Reader on the IBM enables the blind to hear computer output as speech. The blind person hears the words on a computer display, which are read with voice output. The *Xerox-Kurzwell Personal Reader* converts print to audible English, enabling the visually impaired to read newsprint and books.

Alternative Keyboards

Alternatives to the conventional keyboard include membrane keyboards, keyguards, and switch controls. Membrane keyboards contain touch-sensitive sectors that can be programmed like keys or with messages.

Voice-controlled keyboards are becoming more available for use in engineering and other professions. It seems reasonable to expect that this alternative will be available in schools in the next few years.

Multimedia Instruction

The computer, video, audio, and even satellite are becoming synthesized into one multimedia device. The computer can now replace most of the stand-alone equipment used by teachers as audiovisual aids. As an integrated tool, the computer as a multimedia device can be used in many ways for instruction.

Presentation

Teachers can use the computer and special overhead projectors to make any kind of presentation using graphics, moving video, slides, and overheads.

Digitizer

Still photographs, drawings, and videotape can be digitized, stored on computers as files, and used in presentations and other forms of instruction.

Printer

Whether printing to the screen or on paper, the printing capabilities of computers are enormous. The font, style, size, and other features of text can be readily changed for any instructional purpose or to enhance the appearance of text. And, of course, the graphics capabilities are enormous (see later section).

Videodisc

The videodisc can contain 54,000 single slides on a disk and up to one hour of running video. The videodisc is read with a laser beam; the reflection off pits in the disc generate video signals, which in turn create video and sound. Videodiscs can be used in the same way as videotapes and can be controlled by a computer, creating interactive video. A video frame or sequence of frames can be instantly and randomly accessed. A great assortment of videodiscs are commercially available and most of them can easily be turned into computerized instruction or used for group instruction.

Compressed Video

Compressed video is optically stored or digitized video signals on a CD-ROM or hard disk of a computer. Phillips International and Sony have developed a system called *compact disc interactive* (CD-I); Intel has *digital video interactive* (DVI); and IBM has introduced *M-Motion*. The DVI system provides applications including training, tutorials, and storage of information. These technologies may replace videodisc and further solidify the computer as a multimedia device for entertainment, education, and communications.

Based on television technology to compress and decompress video signals, the system compresses and decompresses video at 30 frames per second. The effect is like a videotape. With a camera or videotape source, the computer digitizes sequences on hard disk or CD. The video can be enhanced using graphics and special effects. Because video can be converted to a computer signal, compressed video will reduce costs of video productions and offer lower overall costs, and computers combined with videophones will provide cheaper and widely available distance education and better communications. This technology may supplant videotapes and audiodisks and enable schools to produce their own instructional materials that can be delivered on computer.

CD-ROM

A 12-cm (4 11/16 in.) compact disc/read only memory (CD-ROM) stores 550 megabytes of information or the equivalent of 270,000 typed pages of text. The CD-ROM is aluminum coated with plastic. A new version called the "single-play" is smaller, about 3 1/8 in., and contains 180 megabytes. The CD-ROM provides storage and access to text, graphics, and audio, through a laser converting information through a photosensor. For now, the primary use of the CD-ROM seems to be for storing published products and as an information storage and distribution medium. Students can have a research library in a box, and there is much promise for the CD in the classroom.

GEODISC, produced by Geovision of Norcross, Georgia, provides maps that can zoom down to an area the size of one city block. *SCIENCE HELPER K-8*, produced by PCC-SIG of Sunnyvale, California, has 1,000 science and mathematics lesson plans. If schools start to purchase these products in greater quantities, the market for CD-ROM applications will increase and provide students and teachers with many alternatives in learning and research.

Graphics

In the last few years the more powerful microcomputers have made graphics available to pupils and teachers for many uses in the classroom. Now it is possible to make sophisticated drawings, charts, and artwork and to merge them with products of various kinds. Classroom teachers can use graphics programs with the visual arts, and these programs can be used in design, drafting, and any other part of the curriculum that requires this capability.

Most good word-processing programs incorporate some form of built-in graphics capability for simple illustrations. But there are some good special graphics programs that provide near-professional work, such as *Harvard Graphics*. Most graphics programs can make it possible to expand, shrink, flip, rotate, copy, paste, and move objects on the screen with an array of "tools" in the software. The simplest graphics programs are called *draw programs*, such as *PC PaintBrush* and *MacDraw*. With a draw program almost any geometric shape can be formed. More complex are *paint programs*, such as *PC PaintBrush* and *MacPaint*, which permit filling in sections with different shades, hues, and colors. In painting, as in drawing, the experience is manually closest to using a pencil or pen to make drawings, except that the product is displayed on a screen and saved digitally. The most complex graphics programs are some form of computer-aided design (CAD), which has replaced traditional drafting. Used in drafting, engineering, and architecture, CAD increases productivity and reduces the labor in drawings traditionally done by hand.

Desktop Publishing

Originated by Xerox Corporation in the 1970s, desktop publishing is one of the most revolutionary advances in printing since the printing press and the computer. Using windows, icons, a mouse, pointers, and graphics, Apple Computer introduced desktop publishing to the market for the Macintosh. Now there are several programs for Macintosh and IBM computers. These programs have revolutionized printing, enabling some small companies to produce high-quality books and other publications without the expense and overhead traditionally associated with a large printing house.

Desktop publishing programs were developed to work with word-processing and graphics programs, although it is possible to use the text and graphics capability of the program itself. The characteristics of a desktop program are (a) text composition similar to printer's typesetting, (b) combination of text and graphics, (c) editing capability, and (d) high-resolution printing.

There are now many desktop programs on the market, but two of the oldest and most expensive are *PageMaker* and *Ventura Publisher*. Both are available for Macintosh and IBM computers. *PageMaker*, the first desktop program, is considered to be easy for beginners to learn and is especially useful in making newspapers, newsletters, and pamphlets. *Ventura Publisher* was developed by the Xerox corporation and is highly regarded by evaluators.

Although desktop publishing may be used in some schools to produce newsletters or the school yearbook, it may also have a wide range of applications in regular classrooms, depending on the imagination of the teacher. A desktop publishing program can teach skills beyond the obvious one of creating a printed product. Students who engage in group project-oriented activities must plan together, work as a team, and engage in the kind of give-and-take that characterizes the modern workplace.

The elements of desktop publishing concern text, graphics, and page design or layout. A pupil can select text or font types and styles in the desktop program or incorporate text fonts from word-processing programs. There are literally scores of text sizes and styles available. Most programs include special characters, foreign language, and scientific notations.

Voice/Speech Synthesis

Special software and cards for the computer can cause a computer to create a human-sounding voice in response to commands or to printed text. Mentioned in the literature as a communications aid for handicapped, blind, or speechless children, it can also be used to read to young children. As the costs continue to drop and power increases, there will be more uses of voice in computers, which may be stimulated by the increasing elderly population who could benefit from the same functions as handicapped children. It is technically possible for voice programs to "read" text to children in English or any foreign language as part of an instructional activity.

Support for the Teacher

The typical teacher in elementary school and a few in secondary schools and college will use instructional devices in addition to lecture. Lectures traditionally have been conducted by the teacher with commercial or teacher-made materials. The microcomputer now provides thousands of software programs that teachers may use for instruction.

Drill

One of the first types of instructional software was the so-called drill program. Typically, it was developed for arithmetic drills, such as multiplication combinations, and was often based on a game format or simply a very boring rote memorization technique. Unfortunately, because these programs were so easy to produce and dominated the market in the early days of microcomputer software, the drill program came to characterize computers in education for many people. Today, the computer software is much better and improving, but the "bad reputation" of the early drill programs still lingers. Despite the criticism of drill packages, some programs are very effective for certain children who may need to overlearn facts. It may be true that the computer is an expensive way to provide "flash cards" to a child, but it may actually be more economical and reliable than having a teacher or peer engage a pupil in this kind of activity.

Tutorial

A more sophisticated use of the computer is as a tutorial device, and it is here that the long-term hope for computers in school may be realized. As mentioned earlier, the most effective type of instruction is tutorial instruction, which can result in an average of the 98th percentile, or two standard deviations above the mean, compared to conventional instruction. As computers begin to incorporate more tutorial instruction with digitized video, virtually any pupil should be able to receive any kind of tutorial instruction on any subject. This is the basis for hope that education can provide individualized instruction. Tutorial programs in the military have been remarkably effective—learning is faster and retention is greater. Any classroom may have a range of students with abilities spanning several grade levels. The best a teacher can hope to accomplish with group instruction is to address the needs of the majority of students in the middle range of abilities. With tutorial programs, individualized needs of all students can be met.

Simulation

This is a highly effective way of introducing pupils to interesting tasks that would be impossible or difficult in any traditional classroom. Simulations in science, such as flying, charting a flight to the moon, or doing science experiments, are very popular. Simulations in social science are also popular, such as one called the *Oregon Trail*, which requires participants to plan carefully for a trip in a covered wagon and to deal with emergencies and exigencies along the way.

Expert System

Expert systems are being developed in many disciplines, and some can already be reliably used to perform tasks, such as diagnose certain diseases. Based on the skills and knowledge of human experts, an expert system is an effort to imitate or simulate the reasoning processes of the human expert. Expert systems may become available in educational applications for use in teaching students to understand and master areas of the curriculum that may be beyond the expertise of their teachers.

Testing

Formative testing is important in mastery learning and could be a boon to individualized and cooperative learning models. Time constraints limit the ability of any teacher to provide highly individualized teaching, and formative testing—assessments made continually and daily—is not attempted. A computer could provide virtually any kind of daily testing, tracking, reporting, and recommendation for learning or remediation.

Cooperative Learning

Cooperative-learning models are spreading in education because it is believed that achievement increases when a student works as a member of a small team. The workplace is also based on cooperative work groups and may be part of the reason that schools are accepting this model for instruction. The computer can be a resource and productivity tool for a team of cooperative learners, supporting their research and providing production tools for products.

Individualized Learning

This has been addressed earlier under Tutorial, but it bears repeating that proper use of computers and instructional software can provide individualized instruction for any pupil. The computer could be developed to permit highly specific objectives to be managed for each student.

Reporting, Grading, and Record Keeping

Systems for electronic storage and transfer of data about students, grades, and other information can be entered into a teacher's computer in the classroom and retained for the teacher's use. Any file can then be transmitted to the principal's office and to the central office. Reports could be collected, as needed, quickly and efficiently, without the interference that so often accompanies such activities. Many times, for example, a survey or form will be needed. After completing and turning in the information, a new form will be needed on a slightly different topic in a week or so, much of it the same as the first document. When the information is stored in databases, schools can generate reports without the labor now involved.

Instructional Learning System (ILS)

There are a few companies that develop ILS products for schools. These are usually "turnkey" systems, including hardware and software in one bundle. They are comprehensive and usually quite expensive. Most such systems have been purchased with federal grant support. For the cost of one or two ILS classrooms, most schools could equip most of their classrooms with computers and software. Although ILS programs are comprehensive and may contain all subject matter, tracking software, testing, and management, it remains to be seen if many schools will decide to invest in such systems on a large scale or elect to install different kinds of curriculum integration models.

Uses of Telecommunication Functions

Teachers can and should use the telecommunication functions of computers. With very little additional expense, a new world of information and instantaneous long-distance communication is made available to students, providing actual experience of the global economy and its required skills.

In addition to a suitable computer, a school will need a modem and appropriate telecommunications software. The physical connection of a modem to a computer is relatively simple. A modem connects to a telephone line, however, which can block incoming calls unless the connection is to a dedicated telephone line. Many software packages are available for modems, including *ProComm Plus*, *Kermit*, and *CrossTalk*. If computers in a school are connected to a network, the modem and software can be shared by more than one classroom.

Bulletin Boards

An electronic bulletin board is the computer-age equivalent of a bulletin board in a public building. People may leave notes, information, advertisements, announcements, and a variety of items.

Computer bulletin boards are numerous and are usually established by people who want to share information. Some corporations, especially computer-related companies, have set up informational bulletin boards for their customers who can ask for information, get help, and leave suggestions. Some computer users "chat" with one another over the modem, much like ham radio operators. Some romances have even blossomed through computer connections.

Teachers can establish local bulletin boards for students to use as a means of teaching them practical skills about using telecommunications and for social and instructional activities. For example, a 6th-grade bulletin board might be set up among all 6th-grade classrooms in the school district. Part of the classroom work and projects might involve sharing information among the students of various classrooms. Other than the initial investment for the modem and software, in addition to the computer and a telephone line, there is no cost for such applications as long as only local telephone calls are made.

On-Line Services

On-line services fall generally into three categories: information, transaction, and communications. Information can range across many subjects, from airline routes and timetables to zip codes and scientific knowledge bases; there are currently about 4,000 such databases worldwide that can be accessed through a computer. If desired, one can buy almost anything on-line, and transaction services include banking, brokerage services, and travel—it is possible to make hotel reservations, arrange car rentals, and book tours from a computer.

Some on-line databases are used for instructional activities, but there is a fee involved, although some vendors offer educational discounts. Dialog offers low-priced services to schools; Dialog's CLASSMATE services provide subject matter-information in 320 databases. GTE offers WorldClassroom for science information about earthquakes and weather. The National Geographic has Kids Network, subsidized by the National Science Foundation, to give pupils a chance to participate in scientific experiments. Although some services would be inappropriate for the classroom, teachers may want to use newspaper-article and encyclopedia services available in databases.

Here are some of the popular on-line services:

- *CompuServe:* Offers financial data, electronic shopping, and networking for businesses.
- *Dialog:* Offers 390 databases that have 270 million references from 100,000 publications.
- *Dow Jones News:* Provides general news and sports information and specific financial information and services.
- *GEnie:* General Electric's GEnie has over 100 services.
- *GTE Education Services:* Includes mail, bulletin boards, and databases.
- *LinkNet Inc.:* Links teachers with other teachers locally and nationally through two networks and includes notes, techniques, and databases.
- *Long Distance Learning Network:* AT&T's offering links teachers and students around the world by matching those with similar interests.
- *Prodigy:* A new on-line service offered by Sears and IBM, this is a general-purpose data service that is strong on transactions.

Voice Mail

Some schools use voice mail to connect parents with recordings about homework, assignments, and general school information. By selecting items on a "voice bulletin board," parents can learn about the sale of tickets, parent meetings, activities, and other important information. Some schools use voice-activated systems to call homes to report truancies, and parents can leave voice recordings for teachers.

FAX Machines

FAX (from *facsimile*) machines are fast becoming as popular with the American public as VCRs and answering machines for telephones. There is a range of options available, from very inexpensive units to "intelligent" FAXs and FAXs built into computer systems. Some version of the FAX may someday replace services of the U.S. mail for ordinary citizens, and it is certain that FAXs will either become "smarter" from computerization or be a feature of some computerized device. Even now, a FAX can be an interesting tool for pupils to use in a language-arts learning activity by communicating with other classrooms.

Local-Area Network

One of the fastest growing trends in businesses is microcomputer networking. As mentioned earlier, some schools are developing networks similar to those used in American businesses for improved communications and economical use of resources. Networks are popular in small companies, but even *Fortune* 1000 companies are turning to local-area networks. Purchases of local-area network (LAN) hardware and software are on the upswing in finance, banking, transportation, and service industries, and some schools are beginning to establish microcomputer networks. The mainframe computer may become obsolete in this decade as a result of advances in networks and increases in the speed and power of microcomputers.

Networks are physically connected by cables and controlled by standardized communications known as *protocols*. There is sometimes confusion between LANs, switched labs, networked labs, and Integrated Learning Systems (ILS). Switched labs are computers connected for the purpose of sharing printers. The most common types (topologies) of LAN systems are the *Ring* and *Bus*. LANs are superior to disconnected computers because of the ability to communicate and share software and hardware. Purchasing software for a LAN is often more economical than for several stand-alone units. One significant benefit of a LAN is the ability to transmit electronic mail (e mail), which can increase the professional association of teachers with peers in the building or in other buildings.

Distance Learning

The term *distance education* once referred exclusively to correspondence courses, but it is now almost synonymous with satellite instruction—although radio, speaker phones, electronic blackboards, microwave television, and computer conferencing can also qualify. The two prominent forms of distance education, which are forms of television, use satellite and fiber-optic delivery.

In a satellite transmission, an uplink transmitter sends a signal to a satellite orbiting the Earth. That signal is returned by the satellite to a downlink (dish), which receives the signal and turns it into a video signal for viewing on an ordinary television set. Satellite technology may be used for instruction and for in-service training of teachers. The costs of receiving installations are minimal: Over 16,000 schools have receiving dishes (Ku-Band, C Band, and Mixed Band receivers), representing an investment of approximately $32 million for less than 1% of America's school buildings. And 10,500 of these schools, or about 65% of those equipped, are single-building K-6, K-8, or K-12 schools.

Satellite instruction is delivered throughout the United States, and there are so many producers that it is now a highly competitive industry. Numerous state education agencies, universities, local school districts, and private vendors provide courses of instruction and other services via satellite for schools. The greatest needs are in rural areas, which lack the comprehensive services of larger districts, but any classroom can participate.

Most satellite instruction is one-way interactive, meaning the students can see and hear the teacher, but the teacher cannot see the students. Voice connections are made through telephone, usually over an 800 "call-in" line. But telephones, computers, video, audio, satellite, fiber optics, and other technologies are correlated and are rapidly becoming integrated. It is possible for one teacher on satellite to interact with as many sites as necessary or feasible. When this application becomes available, it will be extremely cost-effective, especially if planning can be managed at the state and local levels by educators who can meet their own needs.

Hughes Aircraft and the Advanced Communications Corporation (ACC) are promoting digital DBS as a new method of satellite transmission. ACC was the first company to file for digital DBS with the Federal Communications Commission, followed by Hughes, and only Hughes and ACC have the prime locations over the United States approved by the FCC under an international agreement.

The advantages of digital transmission are well-known to NASA and the space communications community. Indeed, deep-space probes would have been impossible without it. Digital transmission allows system design flexibility and a reliability of fidelity that cannot be attained with analog. Telephone distance transmission and switching are rapidly becoming all-digital and the digital local telephone loop is being developed. A DBS transmission capability will provide vast new applications of technology. Digital communication could link voice and data through a single set of standard interfaces. This system promises lower costs, greater speed, and more flexibility. It will be possible to get television and other kinds of digital information through one cable to the classroom.

Although principally used in the most rural states and focusing on higher education, fiber cable is increasingly used for transmission of two-way interactive television courses, meaning that students and the teacher can see and hear each other simultaneously. The state of Maine is an example of such a system. Through fiber connections, a teacher originates a class to students who are located in classrooms throughout the state. Using two monitors, directional microphones, and remote-controlled cameras, all controlled from a menu-driven electronics board, the teacher can see and talk to individual students at each site, and the students can see the teacher and students at other locations.

This trend will grow as fiber-optics becomes more available, involving more K-12 schools. Although entire courses may not need to be delivered, video conferencing would be an ideal way to involve students in state-of-the-art educational activities for many instructional purposes. It is an excellent way to take a "field trip" without leaving the building and an economical way to interview a dignitary.

Portable Databases

Placement of databases on CD-ROMs has given rise to a new industry called *portable databases*. Rather than paying for connection time and possibly long-distance telephone charges while using an on-line database, it is possible to buy CD-ROMs that can be updated regularly.

Technologically Literate Students: Case Scenarios

Technology in the Classroom

As technological products and services become less expensive and more widespread, they will be used increasingly by schools. Certain technological devices may be used in the classroom to reduce the effects of a decaying system of financial support. As government funding decreases, it will become necessary for schools to operate more efficiently with available resources. As mentioned earlier, new ways of thinking about the role of education in society must emerge to deal with accelerated change. New technologies will be applied to the educational process because teachers, parents, and students recognize their value. The transformation with new technologies from the existing education model to new ways of delivering education are exciting for teachers and students.

As technology is integrated with the school curriculum for specific instructional and social purposes, research will focus on the effects of technology on students, their cognition, social interactions, self-esteem, and cooperativeness, the sociology of the classroom, and many other areas. As research and development continue, we will all learn what effects technology will have on the relationships of teachers to their students. We will learn at what ages and in what subjects specific technology can be most effective in carrying instruction and for what types of individuals specific technologies may be most beneficial. For now, we can only speculate about how the role of the teacher might change, but early indications are that technology in the classroom will be interesting, challenging, and enjoyable for both teacher and student. The prerequisite, though, is that the teacher must think of the computer as something to make the job easier rather than just another subject to teach.

In this book, the point has been made that it is possible to achieve success with the majority of students in two ways: with low student-teacher ratios or with technologically delivered instruction. The cost of teachers (labor-intensive system) is expensive and has low productivity. The costs of a computerized curriculum, although initially high, can actually reduce instructional costs and keep them down, as technology has reduced costs and increased productivity in other industries. Interactive technology provides a reciprocal dialogue between the user and the system. Unlike a lecture or a videotape, where the learner sits passively, absorbing only a fraction of the information offered, interactive instruction requires the student to become actively involved and increases attention span, feedback, achievement, and retention.

The use of technology is an important goal of education for two reasons: first, because of its potential impact on teaching and learning and, second, because modern institutions need to incorporate technologies. Cost-effectiveness and improved productivity can be realized in education if technology can improve student achievement significantly. Coupling technology with the mastery–learning or tutorial models of teaching may approach the "two-Sigma level" described by Bloom.

In many conventional classrooms, where pupils spend 90% of the time listening to teachers talking, bright students are often bored and slower students do not get help. This is an inefficient way to teach. In all the criticism about education, this context has been largely overlooked.

By using the same space (see Figure 7.1) but arranging it differently—with workstations, computer terminals, and a duplicating and resource area—and structuring learning assignments so that children—as individuals and in small groups—construct their own learning, the teacher is able to achieve individualized learning and cooperative learning.

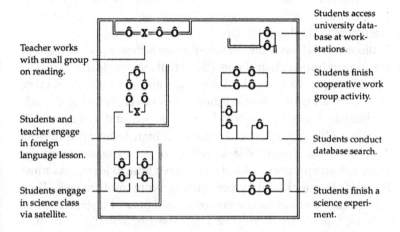

Figure 7.1. Restructured Classroom

The teacher must alter the physical space of the classroom, change customary routines, and put the emphasis on individual and small-group responsibility. The capabilities of the computer as a multimedia tool, an individual tool, and the hub of small-group activities are an untapped resource. With a computer and a criterion-referenced test system based on the sequence of skills in the curriculum, it is possible to determine what each student actually knows or can do.

Specific curriculum steps can be identified for the student, instructional approaches tailored, and extraordinary progress made because in the technology-assisted classroom teacher and student are constantly on task, particularly in monitoring achievement toward curricular objectives and in determining instructional plans. Computers can provide the mechanism for improved student achievement.

To improve schools, reform must focus on variables that will make a difference: the teaching and learning conditions of pupils. The predominant model of classroom instruction in teacher training (Rosenshine & Stevens, 1986) is based on correlates of achievement derived from research on teaching behavior presumed to be effective, such as eye contact, types of questions, pauses, examples, and redirection of questions provided by the teacher. However, as mentioned earlier, group instruction as practiced in most classrooms is highly ineffective.

Bloom (1984) advocates *replacing group instruction* with mastery learning or tutorial instruction. Recall that mastery learning results in achievement one standard deviation above a traditional class, that tutorial instruction (1 teacher to 4 or fewer students) exceeds traditional classes by two standard deviations, and that most children in public schools could achieve at high levels with tutorial instruction. Students who lack aptitude or perseverance need to be taught at an appropriate level, must have time to learn, and must be carefully monitored before moving on to another task. They cannot survive poor instruction or a rapid pace of instruction.

What follows are descriptions of classroom activities and other school functions that incorporate technologies. Rather than dwelling on research and designs and research variables, this chapter presents a series of scenarios to provide glimpses of how technologies can be used for teaching, learning, and administration.

Imagine classrooms where students construct their own learning projects and find their own way to the right sources of information. Imagine that the schools are connected, tied into the great information network that surrounds and envelops the world. Children at all age levels daily engage in "projects" that stimulate critical thinking and help them develop problem-solving skills they need for the new century. Imagine teachers who are able to collaborate with one another via computer and students who are able to collaborate with peers in other classrooms, other schools, or around the world. Computers and telecommunication permit access to the world outside with a free flow of information in and out. Imagine, also, that these children have access to these resources from home or from the study areas in the school. At night, when children are doing homework, they can get on-line assistance.

First Grade

The children arrive on a rainy day and remove their rain gear and boots. They enter the classroom and immediately go to work without being told what to do while Ms. Lynn, their teacher, talks quietly with one of the parents. The classroom is structured on a program-directed system that puts the children in the position of making many decisions for themselves. They all know what is expected, what projects to work on, and who their collaborators are to be.

For example, Jason, whose parents are physicians, learned how to read before coming to school. In other ways, Jason is slow; small for his age with awkward motor patterns, he tends to cry easily. But Jason hurries to the language experience center so he can assist Ramon with the equipment. Ramon's partner, Jennie, sits down next to him. Ramon is taller than Jason and very likable; his mother is often unemployed, and as a single parent with a poor income she has not been able to spend a lot of time with Ramon, but she wants to. He is proud of his progress with the speech therapist in improving his speech sounds. In fact, Ramon and Jason work on some of the same speech sounds together, both of them having difficulty with fricatives. As soon as Jason finishes tutoring Ramon for a few minutes, he moves on to his own assignment in the manipulative center.

Throughout the room children are working in groups of twos or fours on various activities, and some are working on individual assignments. The children have a wide range of abilities, but their individual needs are accommodated in this classroom, and they also work in small groups together. Ms. Lynn is fully aware of the needs and the individual progress in aspects of the school curriculum of each child.

Actually Jason, Ramon, Jennie, and Ms. Lynn all belong to a group of children and other teachers who will be together for three years, after which time the children will move on to a new environment with different teachers. During these three years, they will have a family atmosphere, learning their basic skills, assisting each other, and having the trust and continuity that this atmosphere brings. There will not be the annual painful separations that exist when children abruptly change rooms and teachers, and where everyone must learn new routines and unspoken rules. Jason, Ramon, Jennie, and their classmates will work with a group of people who know them well, and there will be high expectations for all children in the classroom to achieve in academics, to learn a foreign language, and to develop a sense of teamwork and small-group cooperation. Their world will involve books, music, art, and physical exercise, and by the time they are moved on to the next ungraded classroom they will all be experts at operating computers, computer-related equipment, robots, and other gadgets that just amaze their grandparents. This is a rather typical "high-tech, high-touch" classroom.

Junior High

"If the ancient Greeks were so smart, why were they so dumb?" Melissa posed this question to no one in particular, but Maggie heard her and admonished her for making fun of other people. In an effort to defend herself, and a little embarrassed that she had been caught thinking out loud, Melissa tried to explain. "Well, I don't really mean that but, Maggie, I read this on the CD-ROM about one of the ancient Greeks named Anaximenes: 'The earth is flat and floats on the air. The stars are fixed like nails in the crystal-line vault.' That's pretty dumb, isn't it?" She continued, "and I also read where people used to believe you could tell someone's personality by bumps on the head."

Maggie retorted, "It sounds dumb if you believe it today, but it is unfair to judge people of the past by what we know today." Thus Maggie and Melissa begin a conversation that ends in a project for the World History class dealing with philosophy and contrasting it with scientific achievements. Using a database, a word processor, a CD-ROM reader, and books in the library, they begin a report that documents the Milesian philosophy of Nature beginning in 600 B.C. and end up with a search for new philosophies that attempt to reconcile modern string theory in particle physics.

The Knee Joint—The Weak Link

Rubin and Jackson, who are friends in junior high, are intensely interested in football. They follow a local college team closely and know a lot about professional athletes, too. Both of them hope to play ball in high school. On Monday, during a conversation about a game over the weekend, they learn that one of their favorite players has a knee injury that will require orthoscopic surgery. Wondering what this is, they conduct a database search on the topic and discover that the premier clinic for such knee surgery is in Columbus, Georgia. With the help of the teacher, they decide to do a report on this type of surgery to satisfy a combined science and English assignment.

They make arrangements to visit with the trainers at the local college, who give them a brief tour of the facilities and show them the training room. They discuss the rehabilitation program used by athletes recovering from surgery, but they want to know more. They obtain a videotape from the clinic in Columbus showing the anatomy of the knee, the damage, and the surgical procedure used to correct it. They want to include this in the report, so they get assistance digitizing parts of the videotape on a hard disk. Using a time-base corrector to make the video run properly and confining the video to one-quarter of the screen, they decide to put the written report onto the computer as well. They put in an option for the reader to use when going through the materials if the reader wants to see running video of the knee's anatomy and/or the surgery. They also create some graphics to illustrate the program, selected from a "clip art" program on the school's fileserver network to the classroom computer. Rubin and Jackson may still play football, but they may also be interested in anatomy, kinesiology, medicine, and rehabilitation.

Hola, Mexico

A group of elementary students in Spanish class are excited because today is their weekly visit with their amigos in Mexico. Each

Wednesday the children are connected for conversations with school children in Mexico City. On alternating weeks, they speak English and Spanish, each group helping the other with their language skills. Today it is time to speak in Spanish: Brian and Beth have the major responsibility for coordinating conversation on this end, and Juan and Maria are responsible on the other end.

The classes are connected with the AT&T VideoPhones, which produce high-quality sound and live pictures of the students. Brian and Beth have to explain to the class in Mexico about the way Americans celebrate Christmas. Next week Juan will ask about American football and how it contrasts with *el futbol* in Mexico.

The Interferometer Project of the Ninth Grade

The students are interested in astrophysics. As background, they all read *A Brief History of Time: From the Big Bang to Black Holes* by Stephen W. Hawking, the internationally famous professor at Cambridge University. The students also produce a synopsis of views about the motion of bodies, including those of Aristotle, Galileo, and Newton, and conclude with the work of Einstein about how space takes its shape from the mass it contains. With the help of their teacher, and a scientist who "talks" to them on-line over the communications network using electronic mail, the students learn that a new telescope is being designed to observe space-warping events, and that it is not sensitive to electromagnetic radiation, light, radio waves, or gamma rays but is designed to detect only gravitational waves.

The students want to have the plans for the new telescope, so they can build a mock-up of it to understand how it will work when it is constructed. They obtain data and plans from NASA, get assistance from the teacher as well as from the on-line professor in interpreting the plans, search scientific databases for related topics, and obtain all the information they need. Then, using the graphics and animation capabilities on a cooperative learning-group computer, they design a program that imitates the look and function of the telescope. They design the program so anyone can zoom in to get specific information about parts of the instrument, close-ups, and functional information.

Electronic Art

Jenny heard her brother once say that Vincent Van Gogh was a little weird, but she was really more interested in his painting techniques than any stories about his tumultuous life. She found it hard to believe that he had painted 800 pictures in such a short span of time. Jenny had recently obtained a videodisc from her art teacher that showed all of the works in the Van Gogh Museum in Amsterdam and selected paintings from other galleries. Jenny discovered that by going into extreme close-up mode, she detected the types of brush strokes the artist used.

Jenny and a friend, Jill, began trying to imitate the strokes. They found that there were some common traits throughout the paintings and found, by arranging them in chronological order, that there was a distinct change in strokes over time. Excited by this discovery, they ask the teacher for a videodisc of paintings from the Prado Museum in Spain and one from Paris to compare Van Gogh with other artists.

Sarah Simpson Goes to School

Sarah is an 8-year-old with cerebral palsy. Although very bright, she has difficulty controlling her speech but has good control of her right hand, which is affected by an athetoid condition. She needs to be in a wheelchair most of the time, but until she entered school after moving to the new school this year, her parents were more worried about her ability to communicate than her mobility. In her previous school, she could not talk with her peers or answer teachers' questions. But this school district has a central office staff for the evaluation of all handicapped children who will benefit from technology, working in cooperation with a university faculty.

A special keyboard and communications board has been developed for her that uses a speech generator. It has macros built in for many common responses. Using a communications program called *Living Center* from Words Plus in Sunnyvale, California, she can write and speak using a speech synthesizer from Speech Plus. The synthesizer and a small palmtop personal computer are mounted on the wheelchair to meet all of her communications needs.

* * *

Despite the many criticisms of American education and the attempt to initiate a variety of reforms, it seems clear that the future will reveal that the most important domestic issue for education will be dealing with a knowledge-based economy and the information and media that generate wealth. As Toffler (1991) indicates, this is a change so revolutionary it cannot be mapped by conventional political cartography. He predicts that the new wealth-creation system will force politicians, activists, and political theorists to rethink all political ideas developed during the smokestack era. The current reform movement was inspired by fear of technological and economic inferiority to Japan and Europe. When it is finally recognized that electronic computing technology is more important than Japanese or German manufacturing, the uses of computers will be rapidly expanded in American education to keep the nation competitive. Children in the near future will learn with and from computers, and they will earn their living with computers after they complete school. The progress that has already been made in many U.S. schools to computerize will make future planning much easier. The principal as instructional leader of the school can do much to not only improve education with computers, but also to strengthen America's economic future.

Annotated Bibliography

Bloom, B. S. (1984). The search for methods of group instruction as effective as one-to-one tutoring. *Educational Leadership, 41,* 8.

This article describes the different levels of achievement obtained in conventional, mastery-learning, and tutorial instruction. The contention is made in this text that tutorial instruction, which is the best, can only be realized through use of technology.

Collins, A. (1991, September). The role of computer technology in restructuring schools. *Phi Delta Kappan,* pp. 41-56.

This is an excellent article that provides an overview of the major themes in computer technology for the restructured school.

Dodge, H., Brogdan, R., Brogdan, N., & Lewis, R. (1974). How teachers perceive media. *Educational Technology, 14,* 21-24.

Although it is now dated, the article is one of the few that addresses the problems of getting teachers to use media for classroom instruction. The findings are still relevant.

Drucker, P. F. (1989). *The new realities.* Oxford: Heinemann Professional Publishing.

This is one of the best volumes written by anyone to explain the change in the global economy and the implications for managers.

Dwyer, D. C., Ringstaff, C., & Sandholtz, J. H. (1991, May). Changes in teachers' beliefs and practices in technology-rich classrooms. *Educational Leadership*, pp. 45-52.

Outlining the effects of research to change teachers' attitudes toward computers, the article documents how teachers gradually relinquish transmission control to constructivist learning.

Gross, B. (1989). Can computer-assisted instruction solve the dropout problem? *Educational Leadership*, February, 1989, 49-51.

Demonstrating the effects of computers on at-risk students, this article explains the importance of computers to school administrators.

Heinich, R., Molenda, M., & Russell, J. D. (1989). *Instructional media.* New York: Macmillan.

This is an excellent basic text on the variety of media in the classroom, including computers.

Higgins, J. J. (1990). Computer report card. *The technology revolution comes to education.* New York: McGraw-Hill.

Higgins has provided an interim report of the progress of computers in American education.

Kemmis, S. (1985). Action research and the politics of reflection. In D. Boud (Ed.), *Reflection: Turning experience into learning* (pp. 139-162). New York: Nichols.

A new trend in teacher education is called reflective teaching, and it seems likely to emerge as a predominant model in teacher training throughout the nation. This is an excellent overview of the topic explaining what it means.

Kozma, R. B., & Johnston, J. (1991, January/February). The technological evolution comes to the classroom. *Change*, pp. 10-23.

This is a thorough, concise overview of the impact of technology in classrooms.

Niemiec, R., Blackwell, M., & Walberg, H. J. (1986, June). CAI can be doubly effective. *Phi Delta Kappan*, pp. 750-751.

Using a set of criteria to accept and examine effects of educational innovations, this article reveals the superiority of computerized instruction in terms of cost-effectiveness.

Office of Technology Assessment, Congress of the United States (1989). *Power on! New tools for teaching and learning.* Washington, DC: Government Printing Office.

Although somewhat dated now, this publication of the U.S. Congress is an excellent overview of the uses of technology in educational settings conducted by the Office of Technology Assessment.

O'Malley, C. (1989, October). Where PCs are part of the furniture. *Personal Computing,* pp. 122-124.

O'Malley provides a crisp description of classrooms where computers are only tools used in classrooms rather than the center of attention.

Perelman, L. J. (1991). Restructuring with technology: A tour of schools where it is happening. *Technology and Learning, 2*(4), 30-37.

Perelman provides descriptions of various classroom settings where technological applications are being explored.

Rosenshine, B., & Stevens, R. (1986). Teaching functions. In M. C. Wittrock (Ed.), *Handbook of research on teaching* (3rd ed.). New York: Macmillan.

This is one of the most comprehensive reviews of educational research. It covers a wide range of topics, although technology is only addressed significantly in terms of training.

Stevenson, H. W., & Stigler, J. W. (1992). *The learning gap.* New York: Summit Books.

An interesting book. The authors have summarized the research of several years comparing and contrasting classrooms in Japan, China, and the United States. The distinctions are illuminating.

Thurow, L. (1992). *Head to head.* New York: William Morrow.

The most recent of the "must read" texts about our changing world. Thurow, who is a professor at MIT, defines the economic competition confronting the United States for the next decade.

Toffler, A. (1991). *Power shift.* New York: Bantam.

The most successful of the visionaries, noted for Future Shock and the Third Wave, Toffler has provided a powerful volume covering the impact of the global economy on all institutions.

Wagner, L. (1982). *The economics of educational media*. London: Macmillan Press Ltd.

Cost-effectiveness studies of media in education are very limited, particularly in the United States. This study by Wagner of the economics of educational media in education for Great Britain provides an excellent background for understanding the myriad issues in technology.

Walberg, H. (1991). Productive teaching and instruction: Assessing the knowledge base. In H. Waxman & H. Walberg (Eds.), *Effective teaching: Current research* (pp. 33-62). Berkeley, CA: McCutchan.

This chapter, in addition to the rest of this edited text, provides a comprehensive overview of the statistical analyses of the effects of variables in education.